Paw Prints

Pugs

by Kaitlyn Duling

Bullfrog Books

Ideas for Parents and Teachers

Bullfrog Books let children practice reading informational text at the earliest reading levels. Repetition, familiar words, and photo labels support early readers.

Before Reading

- Discuss the cover photo. What does it tell them?
- Look at the picture glossary together. Read and discuss the words.

Read the Book

- "Walk" through the book and look at the photos. Let the child ask questions. Point out the photo labels.
- Read the book to the child, or have him or her read independently.

After Reading

- Prompt the child to think more. Ask: Have you ever seen a pug? Would you like to play with one?

Bullfrog Books are published by Jump!
5357 Penn Avenue South
Minneapolis, MN 55419
www.jumplibrary.com

Library of Congress Cataloging-in-Publication Data

Names: Duling, Kaitlyn, author.
Title: Pugs / by Kaitlyn Duling.
Description: Minneapolis, MN : Jump!, Inc., 2018.
Series: Paw prints
Series: Bullfrog books | Includes index.
Audience: Ages 5 to 8. | Audience: Grades K to 3.
Identifiers: LCCN 2017041229 (print)
LCCN 2017043183 (ebook)
ISBN 9781624967832 (ebook)
ISBN 9781624967825 (hardcover : alk. paper)
Subjects: LCSH: Pug—Juvenile literature.
Classification: LCC SF429.P9 (ebook)
LCC SF429.P9 D85 2018 (print) | DDC 636.76—dc23
LC record available at https://lccn.loc.gov/2017041229

Editor: Jenna Trnka
Book Designer: Molly Ballanger

Photo Credits: ULKASTUDIO/Shutterstock, cover; Ermolaev Alexander/Shutterstock, 1; Utekhina Anna/Shutterstock, 3; evastudio/Shutterstock, 4; o _ sa/iStock, 5, 23tr; aogreatkim/iStock, 6–7, 23tl, 23br; Africa Studio/Shutterstock, 8–9; Ezzolo/Shutterstock, 10; Dora Zett/Shutterstock, 11; Blue Artist management/amanaimagesRF/Getty, 12–13; Patrick Foto/Shutterstock, 14; HelenWalkerz65/iStock, 15; Juniors/SuperStock, 16–17; Wallenrock/Shutterstock, 18–19, 23bl; India Picture/Shutterstock, 20–21; WildStrawberry/Shutterstock, 22; Eric Isselee/Shutterstock, 24.

Printed in the United States of America at Corporate Graphics in North Mankato, Minnesota.

This book is for the Ballangers and Rocky Joe.

Table of Contents

Small and Stocky

Look at that dog!
What kind is it?

It is small. It is stocky.
It is a pug!

5

A pug has a flat nose.

See its wrinkles?

wrinkles

Its coat is short.

Pet it.

It is very soft.

Some are black.

mask

Others are tan.

They have
a black mask.

tail

Look at that curly tail!

13

Pugs are gentle.

But they like to play!

Pugs also like to nap.

This one snores.

17

A pug is loyal.

It will stay by your side.

Pugs are cute and kind.
They make great pets.
Would you like a pug?

A Pug Up Close

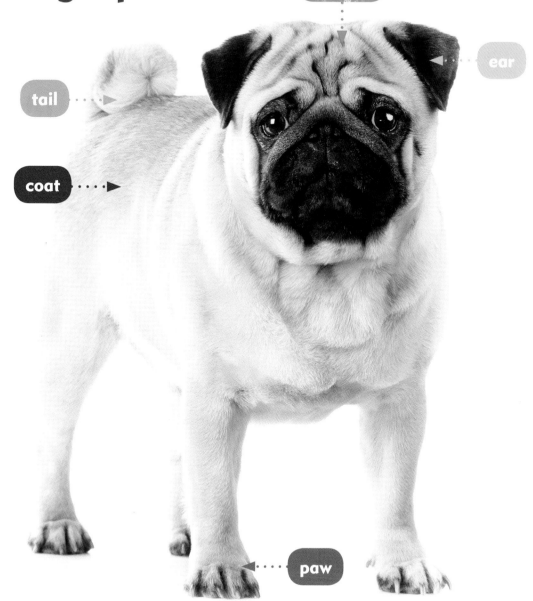

wrinkles

ear

tail

coat

paw

Picture Glossary

coat
A dog's fur.

stocky
Short and sturdy.

loyal
Faithful.

wrinkles
Folds in skin.

Index

To Learn More

Learning more is as easy as 1, 2, 3.

1) Go to www.factsurfer.com

2) Enter "pugs" into the search box.

3) Click the "Surf" button to see a list of websites.

With factsurfer.com, finding more information is just a click away.